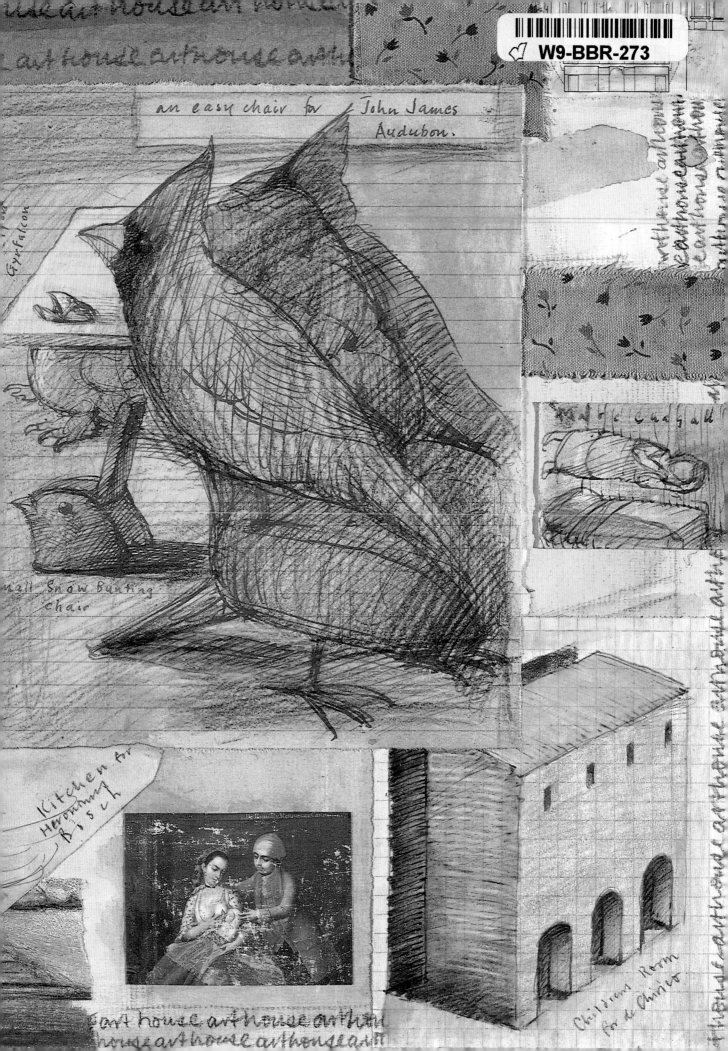

an easy chair for John James Audubon.

Gyrfalcon

Small Snow Bunting chair

Kitchen for Heroming B55L

Children's Room for de Chirico

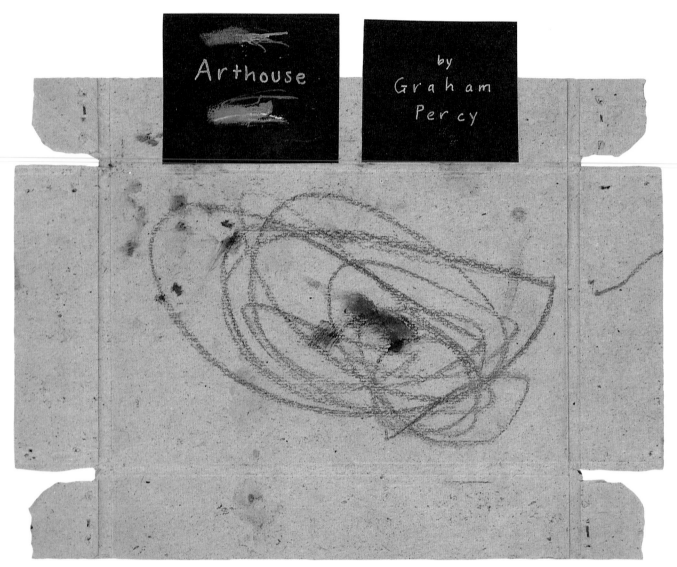

Arthouse

by Graham Percy

Chronicle Books

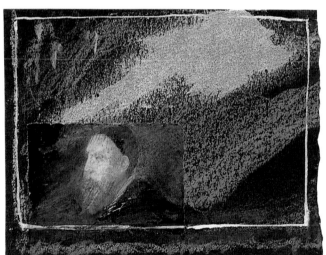

San Francisco

For Mari

Library of Congress Cataloging-in-Publication Data

Percy, Graham.
     ArtHouse / by Graham Percy.
          p.   cm.
     ISBN 0-8118-0497-6
     1. Percy, Graham—Themes, motives.   2. Artists—Influence
     3. Artists—Biography.   I. Title
     NC975.5.P46A4   1994   92-15076
     741.973–DC20   CIP

Printed in Hong Kong.

Distributed in Canada by Raincoast Books,
112 East Third Avenue, Vancouver, B.C. V5T1C8

10 9 8 7 6 5 4 3 2 1

Chronicle Books
275 Fifth Street
San Francisco, CA 94103

Arthouse by Graham Percy

ARTHOUSE / for:
Christo, Hokusai, Munch,
Georgia O'Keeffe, Bosch, Schwitters,
Cézanne, Muybridge, Braque,
Ernst, Kandinsky, Audubon,
Picasso, Piero della Francesca,
Arcimboldo, Klee, Tinguely,
Oldenburg, Cornell, Dürer,
Léger, Calder, Chagall,
Man Ray, Jackson Pollock,
El Lissitzky, Warhol,
Giorgio de Chirico,
Frank Stella,
Grant Wood,
Botero, Johns,
Friedrich,
Kiefer, Rousseau,
Hopper, Piranesi,
Duchamp, Tatlin,
Guston

Christo
Hokusai

Caspar David Friedrich
Attic
Anselm Kiefer
Attic

Johns
Rousseau

Tatlin

Porch
Hopper

Duchamp
Guston

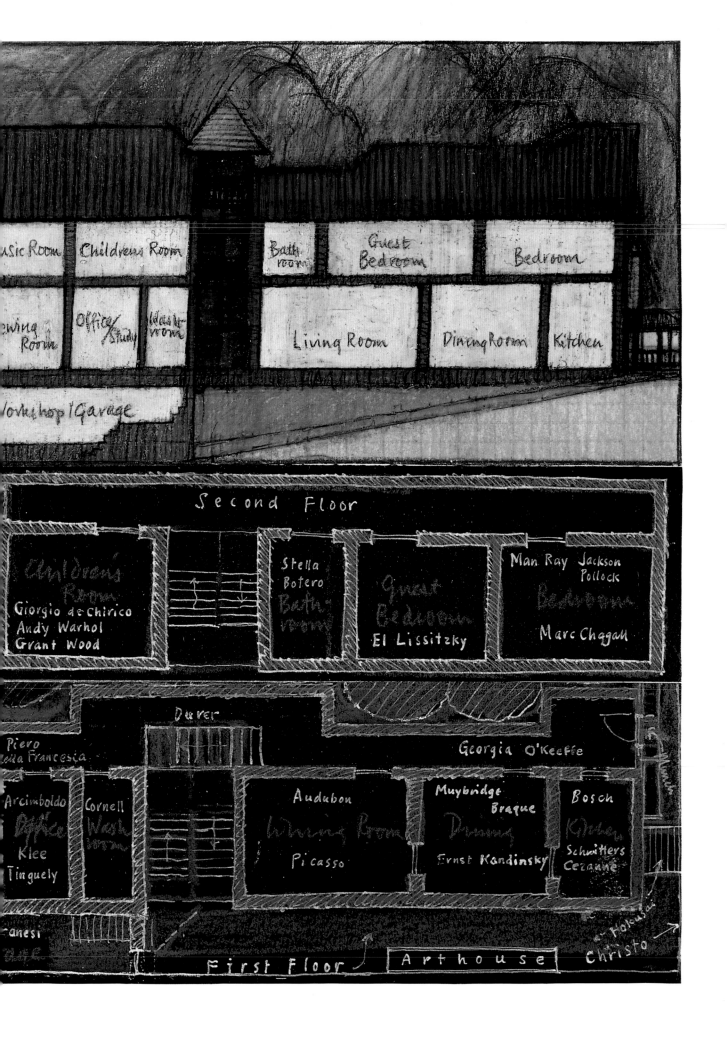

usic Room | Childrens Room

Bath room | Guest Bedroom | Bedroom

ewing Room | Office/Study | Wash room

Living Room | DiningRoom | Kitchen

Workshop/Garage

Second Floor

Childrens Room
Giorgio de Chirico
Andy Warhol
Grant Wood

Stella
Botero
Bathroom

Great Bedroom
El Lissitzky

Man Ray Jackson Pollock
Bedroom
Marc Chagall

Dürer

Piero della Francesca

Georgia O'Keeffe

Arcimboldo
Office
Klee
Tinguely

Cornell
Washroom

Audubon
Living Room
Picasso

Muybridge
Braque
Dining
Ernst Kandinsky

Bosch
Kitchen
Schwitters
Cezanne

anesi

Hokusai
Christo

First Floor → | Arthouse | Christo

A mailbox and garden for Christo

A front porch for Hokus.

A front door for Edvard Munch

A hallway for Georgia O'Keeffe

A kitchen for Hieronymous Bosch

A toaster for Kurt Schwitters

A repigerator for Paul Cézanne

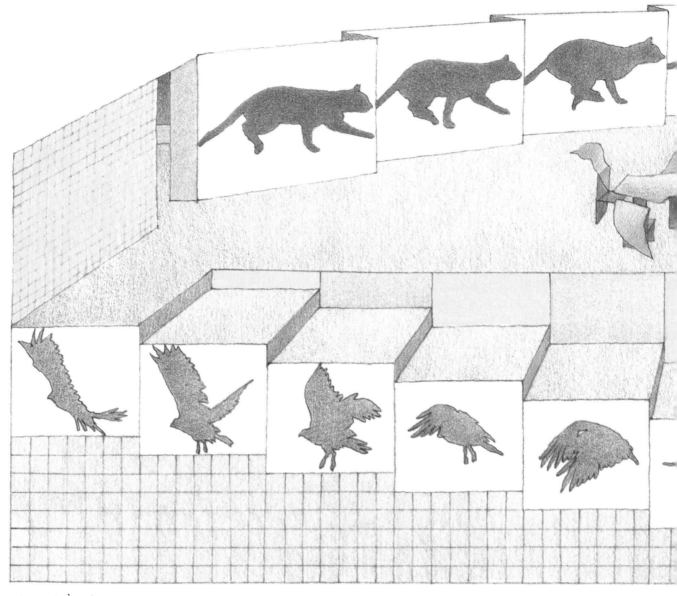

A dining room for Eadweard Muybridge

A dinner table and chairs for Georges Braque

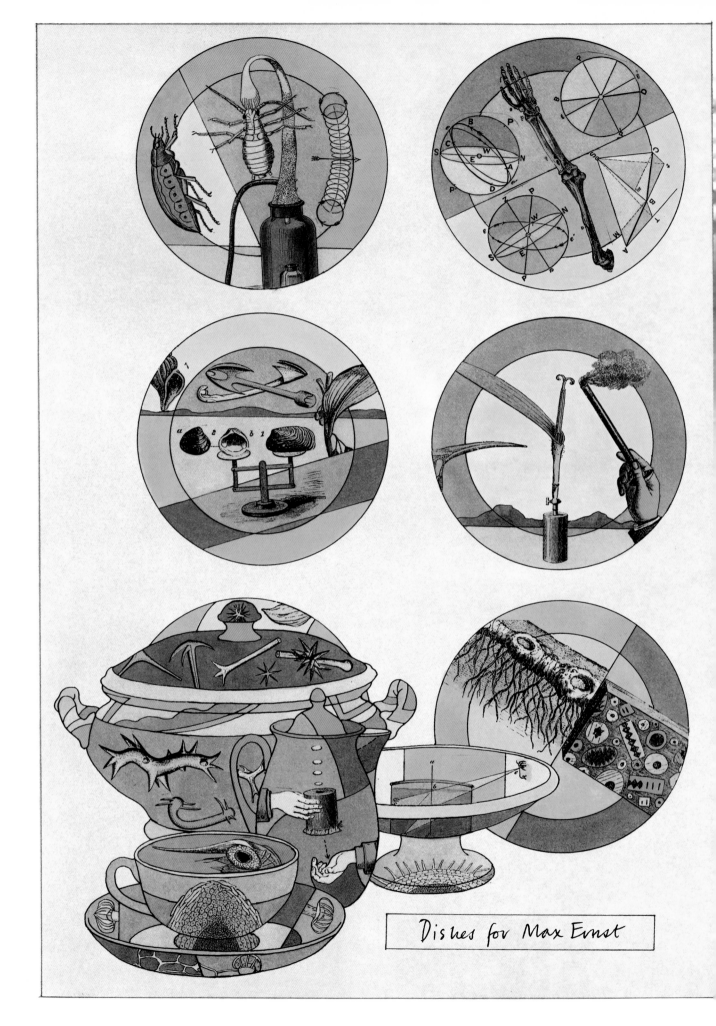

Dishes for Max Ernst

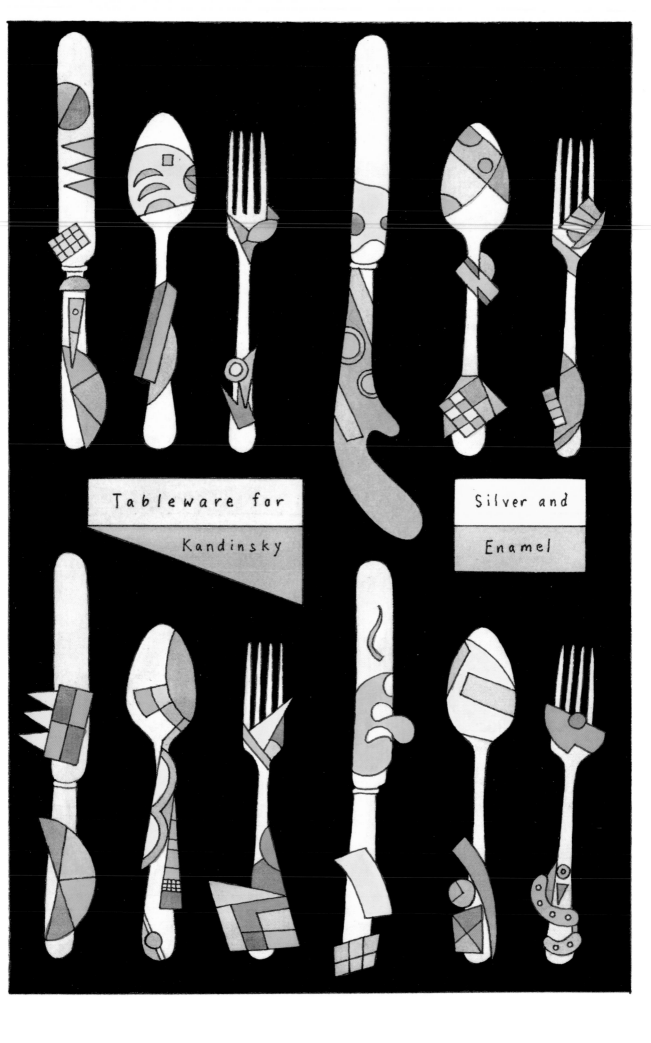

Tableware for

Kandinsky

Silver and

Enamel

A living room for John James Audubon

A couch and TV for Pablo Picasso

Doorway to a study for Piero della Francesca

A study for Arcimboldo

filing cabinet for Paul Klee

A photocopier for Jean Tinguely

A sewing room for Claes Oldenburg

A little bathroom for Joseph Cornell

A staircase for Albrecht Dürer

A music room for Fernand Léger

A piano for Alexander Calder

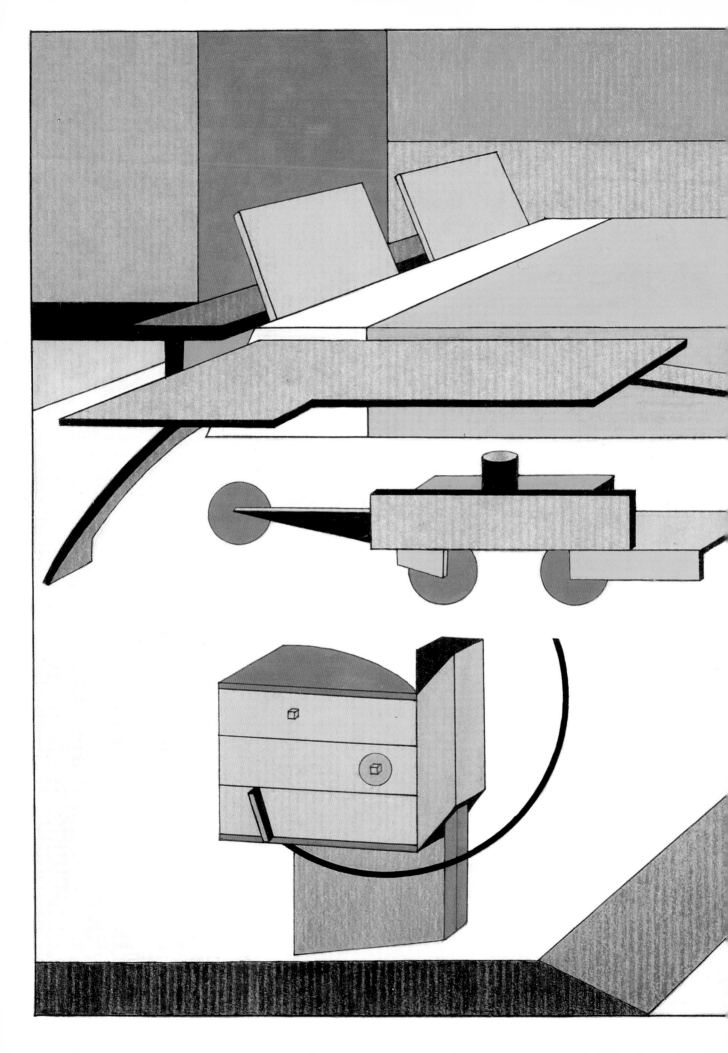

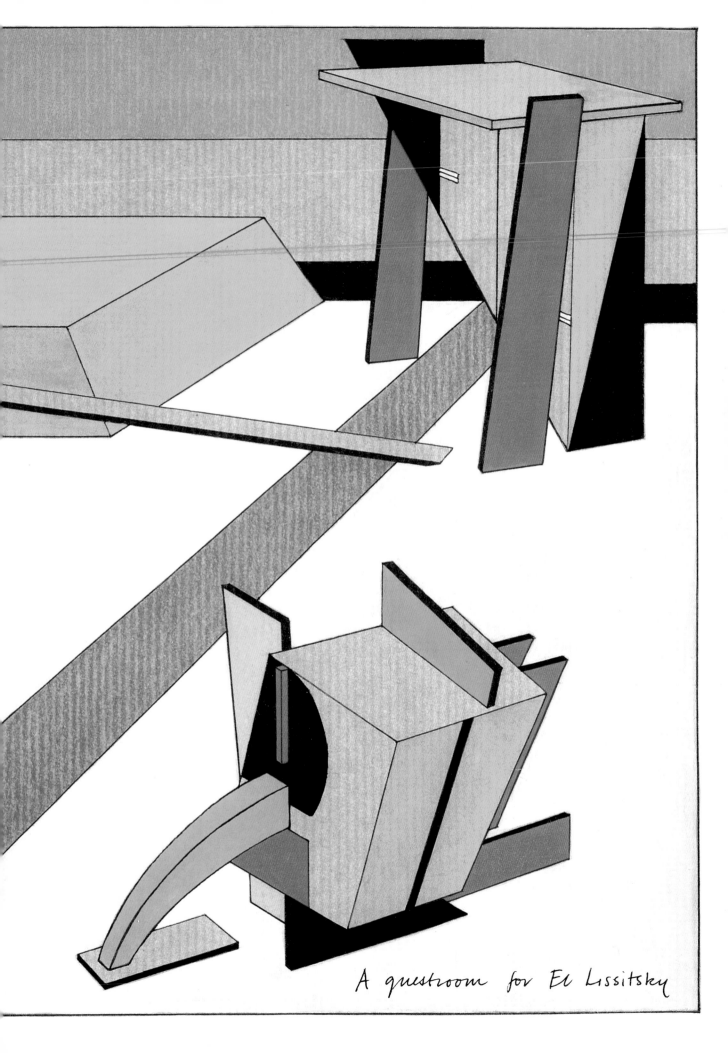

A guestroom for El Lissitsky

A chest of drawers for Man Ray

A wardrobe for Jackson Pollock

A bedroom for Marc Chagall

A children's room for Giorgio de Chirico

A dollhouse for Andy Warhol

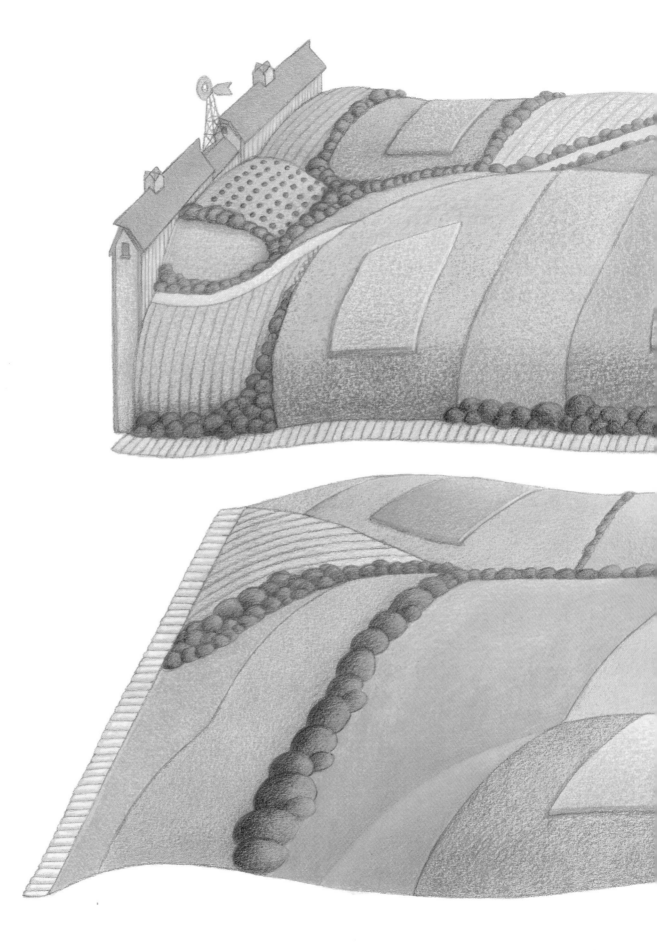

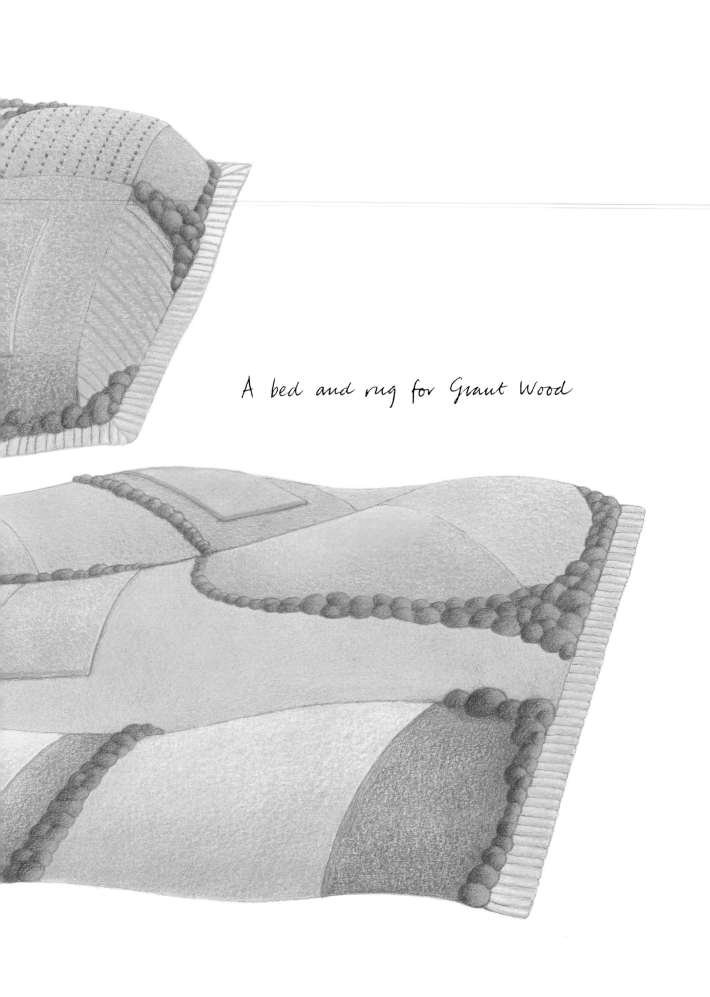

A bed and rug for Grant Wood

A bathroom for Fernando Botero

A linen closet for Frank Stella

A staircase for Jasper Johns

An attic for Caspar David Friedrich and Anselm Kiefer

A window box for Henri Rousseau

A back porch with cacti for Edward Hoppe

A garage and workshop for Piranesi

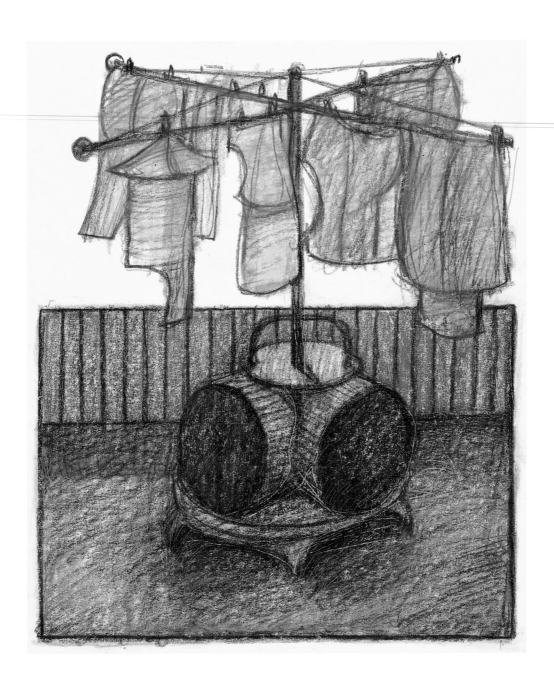

A clothesline for Marcel Duchamp

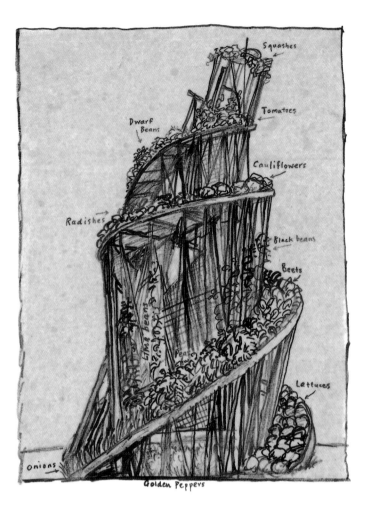

A vegetable patch for Tatlin

A garden shed for Philip Guston

GIUSEPPE ARCIMBOLDO (1527–1593)

The Italian painter renowned for his symbolical
arrangements of fruits, vegetables, animals,
and implements into human forms.
Surrealists revived interest in his work.

JOHN JAMES AUDUBON (1785–1851)

American painter-naturalist. His *Birds of America,*
published in four volumes (1827–1838), is now one
of the most famous and prized books in the world.

HIERONYMOUS BOSCH (*c.* 1450–1516)
Netherlandish painter. His turbulent and grotesque
fantasies are usually allegorical and derived from
biblical texts or proverbs. One of the first artists to
make drawings as independent works.

FERNANDO BOTERO (1932–   )

Contemporary Colombian painter and sculptor. His
delightful vision of everybody and everything as
plump and rounded can be seen in public sculptures
in cities throughout the world.

GEORGES BRAQUE (1882–1963)

French. In 1909, with Picasso, began a new approach
to painting which developed into Cubism. Later
concentrated on still-life and figure compositions.

ALEXANDER CALDER (1898–1976)

One of the first American artists of this century
to achieve international status. All of his work
demonstrates a refined sense of structure and
mechanics as well as wit and lightness of touch.

PAUL CÉZANNE (1839–1906)

French painter whose painstaking analysis of nature made him the greatest of the Post-Impressionists and a key figure in the development of twentieth-century art.

MARC CHAGALL (1887–1985)

Born in Russia, worked mainly in Paris. Most of his subjects were poetic evocations of Russian village life and religious themes. Designed stained glass and sets and costumes for theater and ballet.

GIORGIO DE CHIRICO (1888–1978)

Italian painter, born in Greece. The originator of Pittura Metafisica, or Metaphysical Painting. In the 1930s he abandoned his modern ideals and returned to a form of imitation of the old masters.

CHRISTO (CHRISTO JAVACHEFF) (1935–   )

Born in Bulgaria, worked in U.S. since 1964. His early work, consisting of familiar objects wrapped in canvas or plastics, developed into large-scale landscape installations and wrapped architectural monuments such as the Pont Neuf in Paris (above).

JOSEPH CORNELL (1903–1972)

The great American pioneer and exponent of assemblage. His most characteristic works are his boxes containing found objects—surprisingly juxtaposed.

MARCEL DUCHAMP (1887–1968)

French artist and art theorist. Shocked New York with his *Nude Descending a Staircase* in the Armory Show of 1913. With Picabia led the New York Dada movement. He invented the ready-made (as above).

ALBRECHT DÜRER (1471–1528)

German painter and printmaker. The greatest artist
of the northern European Renaissance. A master
of line engraving and an early experimenter
with the then-new technique of etching.

PHILIP GUSTON (1913–1980)

American, born in Canada. From 1950 one of the major
Abstract Expressionists. After 1970, painted with a deliberate
brutality in a striking comic-book style (as here).

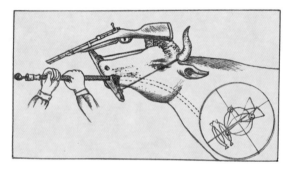

MAX ERNST (1891–1976)

Born in Germany, a French citizen from 1958.
Adapted the techniques of collage and photomontage
to Surrealist uses. Also a sculptor and painter.
Briefly married to Peggy Guggenheim.

HOKUSAI (1760–1849)

The master Japanese printmaker whose surprising views of
life and landscape and dynamic pictorial compositions greatly
impressed and influenced Western painters such as Degas.

CASPAR DAVID FRIEDRICH (1774–1840)

The greatest German Romantic painter.
Introspective and melancholic, his haunting
landscapes have a deep sense of spirituality.

EDWARD HOPPER (1882–1967)

American painter who, in depicting the familiar
and concrete, powerfully conveyed the loneliness
and desolation of life in the big city.

JASPER JOHNS (1930–)

American painter, sculptor, and printmaker. Much
of his work has derived from commonplace two-
dimensional objects—flags, targets, maps. His
sculpture (as above) plays with similarly banal objects.

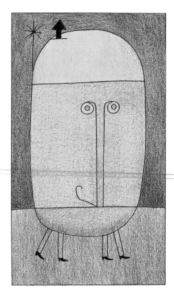

PAUL KLEE (1879–1940)

Swiss painter and etcher. Member of Der Blaue
Reiter group. Later taught at the Bauhaus. One
of the great innovators of the twentieth century.

WASSILY KANDINSKY (1866–1944)

Born in Russia, from 1933 worked in France. One of
the first purely abstract painters and a founder, in 1911,
of Der Blaue Reiter group. Taught at the Bauhaus
from 1922 until it was closed eleven years later.

FERNAND LÉGER (1881–1955)

French painter who developed a Cubist style
based on the geometrical shapes of machinery.

ANSELM KIEFER (1945–)

Contemporary German painter and sculptor. His
paintings and handmade books (above) express
natural forces and magic in their accumulations of
many different materials—lead, earth, straw, etc.

EL LISSITSKY (1890–1941)

One of the best known of the Russian abstract artists.
His work fused Suprematism and Constructivism.

MAN RAY (1890–1977)

American painter, sculptor, and photographer. Lived much of his life in Paris. Several of his works became icons of the Dada and Surrealist movements (as above).

EDVARD MUNCH (1863–1944)

Norwegian painter and printmaker. One of the forerunners of Expressionism. His subjects dealt powerfully with love and death (as in his *Frieze of Life*).

EADWEARD MUYBRIDGE (1830–1904)

Born in England, worked in U.S. Invented a way of photographing animals and humans in motion (as above).

GEORGIA O'KEEFFE (1887–1986)

One of the pioneers of modernism in the U.S. Best known for her sensuous, near-abstract paintings of flowers and plant forms (as above) and for her desert landscapes.

CLAES OLDENBURG (1929–   )

American, born in Sweden. From happenings and environments, his work developed into the soft sculptures of the 1960s. Later came his projects for colossal monuments—using everyday objects.

PABLO PICASSO (1881–1973)

Spanish painter, sculptor, graphic artist, and designer. Studied and lived in France. Perhaps the most famous artist of the twentieth century.

PIERO DELLA FRANCESCA (C. 1420–1492)

Italian. After his death, remembered as a
mathematician rather than as a painter. Now
regarded as one of the greatest artists of his time.

GIOVANNI BATTISTA PIRANESI (1720–1778)

Italian etcher, archaeologist, and architect.
His most original works were his series of
fantastic imaginary prisons (as above).

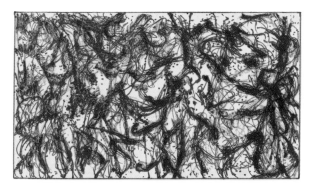

JACKSON POLLOCK (1912–1956)

Arrived at abstractionism in 1940. Invented
"drip" technique of painting and (with Willem de
Kooning) became the most important artist in the
development of Abstract Expressionism in the U.S.

HENRI ROUSSEAU (1844–1910)

French painter. His naive style was much admired
by Picasso and the avant-garde in Paris.
His famous jungle paintings came from books
and visits to the zoo and botanical gardens.

KURT SCHWITTERS (1887–1948)

German painter and sculptor.
Best known for his richly poetic collages.

FRANK STELLA (1936–   )

American. His recent sculptures (as here)
are hectic pattern-mixes of surface and material.

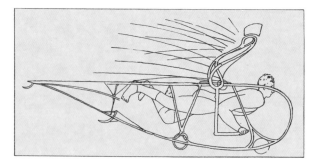

VLADIMIR TATLIN (1885–1953)

Russian. Founder of Constructivism.
His *Monument to the Third International*, never
more than a model, was intended to be higher than
the Eiffel Tower. He also worked on a glider
(above) which he called *Letatlin* (his own name
and the Russian for "to fly").

ANDY WARHOL (1930?–1987)

Painter, graphic artist, and filmmaker. Widely
known and controversial American Pop artist—
famous for his factory methods and use of
repeated photo-based images (as above).

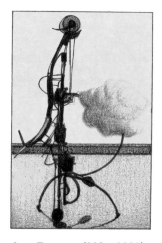

JEAN TINGUELY (1925–1991)

Swiss sculptor. Experimented with movement
and machines. Works in the 1960s were auto-
destructive. He later combined kineticism with
junk sculpture—sometimes involving the spectator.

GRANT WOOD (1892–1942)

American Regionalist painter famous for his
stylized landscapes and the cool humor of
his portraits such as *American Gothic*.

arthouse arthouse arthouse

Christo
mail box

and   plants

Georgia O'Keeffe flower in pot

Picasso T.V

Microwave

Cupboard
space

oranges